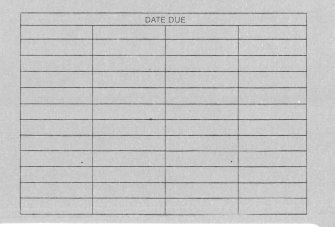

DATE DUE		

WEEKLY WR READER
EARLY LEARNING LIBRARY

My Day at School/
Mi día en la escuela

Getting Ready for School/
Me preparo para ir a la escuela

by/por Joanne Mattern

Reading consultant/Consultora de lectura:
Susan Nations, M.Ed.,
author, literacy coach,
consultant in literacy development/
autora, tutora de alfabetización,
consultora de desarrollo de la lectura

Please visit our web site at: www.garethstevens.com
For a free color catalog describing Weekly Reader® Early Learning Library's list
of high-quality books, call 1-877-445-5824 (USA) or 1-800-387-3178 (Canada).
Weekly Reader® Early Learning Library's fax: (414) 336-0164.

Library of Congress Cataloging-in-Publication Data

Mattern, Joanne, 1963-
    [Getting ready for school. Spanish & English]
    Getting ready for school = Me preparo para ir a la escuela / by/por Joanne Mattern
       p. cm. — (My day at school = Mi día en la escuela)
    Includes bibliographical references and index.
    ISBN-10: 0-8368-7359-9 — ISBN-13: 978-0-8368-7359-7 (lib. bdg.)
    ISBN-10: 0-8368-7366-1 — ISBN-13: 978-0-8368-7366-5 (softcover)
    1. School children—Juvenile literature.   2. Morning customs—Juvenile literature.   I. Title.
  II. Title: Me preparo para ir a la escuela.   III. Series: Mattern, Joanne, 1963- My day at school.
  HQ781.M36418   2007
  372.18—dc22   2006017291

This edition first published in 2007 by
Weekly Reader® Early Learning Library
A Member of the WRC Media Family of Companies
330 West Olive Street, Suite 100
Milwaukee, WI 53212 USA

Copyright © 2007 by Weekly Reader® Early Learning Library

Editor: Barbara Kiely Miller
Art direction: Tammy West
Cover design and page layout: Kami Strunsee
Picture research: Diane Laska-Swanke
Photographer: Gregg Andersen
Translators: Tatiana Acosta and Guillermo Gutiérrez

Printed in the United States of America

1 2 3 4 5 6 7 8 9 10 09 08 07 06

Note to Educators and Parents

Reading is such an exciting adventure for young children! They are beginning to integrate their oral language skills with written language. To encourage children along the path to early literacy, books must be colorful, engaging, and interesting; they should invite the young reader to explore both the print and the pictures.

The *My Day at School* series is designed to help young readers review the routines and rules of a school day, while learning new vocabulary and strengthening their reading comprehension. In simple, easy-to-read language, each book follows a child through part of a typical school day.

Each book is specially designed to support the young reader in the reading process. The familiar topics are appealing to young children and invite them to read — and re-read — again and again. The full-color photographs and enhanced text further support the student during the reading process.

In addition to serving as wonderful picture books in schools, libraries, homes, and other places where children learn to love reading, these books are specifically intended to be read within an instructional guided reading group. This small group setting allows beginning readers to work with a fluent adult model as they make meaning from the text. After children develop fluency with the text and content, the book can be read independently. Children and adults alike will find these books supportive, engaging, and fun!

— Susan Nations, M.Ed., author, literacy coach,
and consultant in literacy development

Nota para los maestros y los padres

¡Leer es una aventura tan emocionante para los niños pequeños! A esta edad están comenzando a integrar su manejo del lenguaje oral con el lenguaje escrito. Para animar a los niños en el camino de la lectura incipiente, los libros deben ser coloridos, estimulantes e interesantes; deben invitar a los jóvenes lectores a explorar la letra impresa y las ilustraciones.

La serie *Mi día en la escuela* está pensada para ayudar a los jóvenes lectores a repasar las actividades y normas de un día de escuela, mientras enriquecen su vocabulario y refuerzan su comprensión. Cada libro presenta, en un lenguaje sencillo y fácil de entender, las actividades de un niño durante parte de un típico día escolar.

Cada libro está especialmente diseñado para ayudar al joven lector en el proceso de lectura. Los temas familiares llaman la atención de los niños y los invitan a leer —y releer— una y otra vez. Las fotografías a todo color y el tamaño de la letra ayudan aún más al estudiante en el proceso de lectura.

Además de servir como maravillosos libros ilustrados en escuelas, bibliotecas, hogares y otros lugares donde los niños aprenden a amar la lectura, estos libros han sido especialmente concebidos para ser leídos en un grupo de lectura guiada. Este contexto permite que los lectores incipientes trabajen con un adulto que domina la lectura mientras van determinando el significado del texto. Una vez que los niños dominan el texto y el contenido, el libro puede ser leído de manera independiente. ¡Estos libros les resultarán útiles, estimulantes y divertidos a niños y a adultos por igual!

— Susan Nations, M.Ed., autora/tutora de alfabetización/
consultora de desarrollo de la lectura

Mom wakes me up early. It is time to get ready for school.

Mamá me despierta temprano. Es hora de prepararse para la escuela.

First, I wash my face and hands.
The warm water and the **bubbles**
in the soap make me feel clean.

— — — — — — — — — — — —

Primero, me lavo la cara y las
manos. Con el agua templada
y las **burbujas** del jabón ya
estoy limpia.

Next, I get dressed. I will wear my purple shirt today. Purple is my favorite color.

Después, me visto. Hoy me pondré mi camisa morada. El morado es mi color favorito.

9

Mom brushes my hair. She makes a ponytail for me.

- - - - - - - - - - - -

Mamá me cepilla el pelo. Me hace una cola de caballo.

Now it is time for **breakfast**.

Cereal and milk are my favorites.

— — — — — — — — — — — — — —

Es la hora del **desayuno**. **Cereal**

con leche es mi desayuno favorito.

Dad helps me learn my spelling words. I spell the words for Dad.

- - - - - - - - - - - - -

Papá me ayuda a estudiar las palabras que tengo que deletrear. Yo le deletreo las palabras a papá.

I brush my teeth after breakfast.

I also wash my hands again.

- - - - - - - - - - - - -

Después del desayuno, me cepillo

los dientes. Además, me lavo las

manos otra vez.

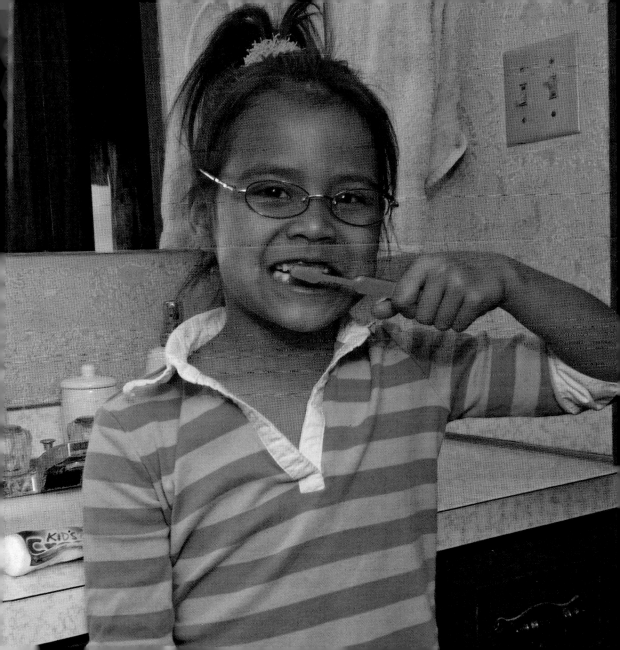

I have all my books and pencils.

I have my **lunchbox**, too.

- - - - - - - - - - - - - - - -

Tengo todos mis libros y lápices.

También tengo mi **lonchera**.

I am ready for school. I know

I will have a good day!

- - - - - - - - - - - - - - - - -

Estoy lista para ir a la escuela.

¡Sé que voy a tener un buen día!

Glossary

breakfast — the first meal of the day

bubbles — balls of air with a thin covering, such as soap, around each one

cereal — a breakfast food made from grains

favorite — something or someone that is liked more than all others

lunchbox — a box with a handle, used to carry food

Glosario

burbujas — globos de aire recubiertos de algo fino, como jabón

cereal — alimento hecho de cereales que se sirve en el desayuno

desayuno — primera comida del día

favorito — algo o alguien que gusta más que todo lo demás

lonchera — bolsa con un asa para llevar comida

For More Information/Más información

Books

Bread and Cereal. Let's Read About Food (series). Cynthia Klingel and Robert B. Noyed (Gareth Stevens)

Brushing Well. Dental Health (series). Helen Frost (Capstone)

Harry Gets Ready for School. Harriet Ziefert (Puffin)

Libros

Get Dressed, Robbie/Vístete, Roberto. Lone Morton (Barron's Educational)

Los cereales. Los grupos de alimentos (series). Robin Nelson (Lerner)

Index

Índice

About the Author

Joanne Mattern has written more than one hundred and fifty books for children. Joanne also works in her local library. She lives in New York State with her husband, three daughters, and assorted pets. She enjoys animals, music, going to baseball games, reading, and visiting schools to talk about her books.

Información sobre la autora

Joanne Mattern ha escrito más de ciento cincuenta libros para niños. Además, Joanne trabaja en la biblioteca de su comunidad. Vive en el estado de Nueva York con su esposo, sus tres hijas y varias mascotas. A Joanne le gustan los animales, la música, ir al béisbol, leer y hacer visitas a las escuelas para hablar de sus libros.